Songs of an Eastern Humanist

Songs of an Eastern Humanist

Edward W. Said

Edited and with an Introduction
by Timothy Brennan

ERIS

ERIS

86–90 Paul Street
London EC2A 4NE

265 Riverside Dr. #4G
New York, NY 10025

ISBN 978-1-916809-97-0

Contents

Introduction

Poetry and music, not the prose for which he later became famous, pushed Edward Said towards the intellectual's life. For many, this may seem surprising. At first glance, Said seems too driven by realism, social conflict, and narrative to bother with the obscure reveries of the inward gaze. On the rare occasions he wrote about poets (in "Yeats and Decolonization", for example, or in his essays on Jonathan Swift) he focused on their fictional or non-fictional prose rather than their prosody. Most of his heroes—the ones to which he continually returns for inspiration—were essayists, satirists, and novelists, just as his favorite critics were theorists of the novel. To think of a typical Said essay on literature, we would likely go to his writing on Conrad's *Nostromo*, Kipling's *Kim*, Melville's *Moby-Dick*, or the long tour de force chapter of *Beginnings* (1975), "The Novel as Beginning Intention". Thinking of his comments on poetry, most would draw a blank.[1]

We forget that his literary critical idol as an undergraduate, R. P. Blackmur, primarily hung out with poets and built his classroom performances around reading their poems aloud, cigarette in hand. The particular themes to which Blackmur gave voice stressed the agonistic role of poetry in a scientific age, which may begin to explain why much of Said's early teaching, most of his passing literary illustrations, and his own (largely private) creative writing were invested in poetry and not the novel at all. When Blackmur points to his most immediate predecessors and rivals, I. A. Richards and William Empson, he focuses on Richards's *Science and Poetry* (1926) declaring that he "was a direct product of a scientific education at Cambridge: he was full of biology, anthropology, and psychology: those great underminers of belief, those great analyzers of experience". The epistemological doubt Blackmur goes on to cherish was less a kind of modern Pyrrhonism (which he singles out for rebuke, since it makes values, not only facts, dubious) than a paradoxical safeguard against the scientific evacuation of all conviction—all sense of justice and right—in the name of control over nature. Poetry for Said, as for Blackmur, was a protest against a culture gullibly enraptured by techno-science.

Blackmur's influence is still evident in Said's class notes for a seminar on language in 1971 at Columbia, where he alternates between the polymathic generalists known as 'philologists', on the one hand, and those, like Roman Jakobson, who were trying to create an "independent science of literature"[2]. As a foil to Jakobson, he opts for the philologists from Jakobsen's Russian milieu: Alexander Potebnja and Alexander Veselovsky. The latter had argued that Western literature's plots and devices had entered Europe by way of Byzantium from the Near and Far East, and that poetry had grown out of folk rituals, popular games, and religious incantations. As for Potebnja, he had been influenced by the great Vichian thinker, Johann Gottfried Herder, arguing that poetic language was the embodied experience of entire peoples. Vico himself had famously claimed (striking a note that Said would take to heart) that the first human language was poetry, not prose.

Blackmur's actual phrasing helps us understand why Said was so intrigued by poetry as compared to other genres. "The arts", Blackmur wrote in 1940, "have more than ever the job of enforcing new tasks upon reason: to show poetry as the wisdom of our violent knowledge—which is what Giambattista Vico said, in 1744, that poetry could do in his great work, *Principi di una Scienza Nuova*, the new way of looking at knowledge"[3]. The work of the poet, he implied, was a sacred task of intellectuals in a world of suffocating market bluster and the pretentious designs of entrepreneurs to bend reality to their will. Although writing at a time when the dark broodings and experimental messianism of literary modernism held sway, Blackmur gave space to the less heralded literary traditions of social conscience and moral action that also became Said's own choices, and a model for his own frankly non-modernist poetry. Blackmur spoke of high modernism's "grasp of the irrational, its techniques of trouble, and its irregular metaphysics—with its fear of syntax, its resort to arbitrary orders, and its infinite sensuality", adding that these "may very well turn out to have been an aberration … The true currents of literature may have flowed purer through other names … Robert Frost rather than Eliot, Robinson rather than Yeats … E. M. Forster's *Passage to India* rather than Joyce's *Ulysses*"—in other words, popular, issues-oriented reformers unafraid of sentiment.[4]

It is in this spirit that Blackmur held up poetry as a way of moving thought to action: "Words are made of motion, made of action or response, at whatever remove; and gesture is made of language—made of the language beneath or beyond or alongside of the language of words"[5]. The statement shored up Blackmur's later observation that poetry is no less than "a criticism of life ... life at the remove of form and meaning; not life lived but life framed and identified"[6]. It is hard to miss here the high purpose which Said was giving to poetry's social role where, among other things, it was a register of one's character. One of Said's students in the early 1970s, the well-known poet David Lehman, recalled that after sending him a long poem titled "The Presidential Years", Said sat down with him to talk it through. "Poetry requires not only rhetorical skill and great intelligence", he said, "but also a 'genuine sensibility' and a connection to the poetry of the past ... Skill could be acquired; sensibility was something you either had or you hadn't"[7].

This is not to say that Said had no doubts about poetry's social effects. In a revealing early essay, "The Still Music of Meditative Poetry" (May 1959), he looks skeptically at himself, throwing out a challenge: "what do poems do" except offer "a vague kind of solace" when so much of the Middle East suffers from hunger and deprivation? For millennia, its defenders have responded that poets are "glorified practical philosophers", "guides to proper action and morals", that they "instruct by pleasing" like "vates, a legislative seer, a model of moral and spiritual refinement". Teetering on the verge at this point in his life when he was still undecided about whether to become a "medical missionary" in the Middle East or a literary critic in his adopted home, he forces himself to face the question. His conclusion was definitely indefinite. It may not feed the hungry, he concluded, but meditative poetry is "a concrete expression of a personal desire for permanent, beautiful satisfaction ... The politics of poetry are the politics of the heart, for better or for worse". He later found another line of reasoning to assuage his doubts by turning to George Makdisi's *The Rise of Humanism in Classical Islam and the Christian West* (1990). "Poetry", Makdisi explained, "pervaded all intellectual products of humanism. Indeed it pervaded all of the divisions of knowledge in the classical Islamic organization of learning"[8].

Said often returned to a small handful of poets who were his companions for solace, rejuvenation, and frequent quotation—especially Gerard Manley Hopkins, W. B. Yeats, Paul Valéry, and, in later life, Constantine Cavafy, Rashid Hussein, and Mahmoud Darwish.[9] Above all Hopkins (whose sprung rhythms and noun-heavy lines he clearly emulates in his own poems) hovers over his entire oeuvre, serving not only as a passage plucked for an occasion, but a guiding presence of mind.[10] In *Beginnings* we learn one reason why—Hopkins's understanding that writing as speaking (as the form of writing that most closely captures direct speech) exists "quite apart from the meaning of what [the author] says", generating a language that is "characteristically his"[11]. On a list of works in progress as a young professor at Columbia University in 1968, he announces that he is writing a "short monograph that attempts to connect directly the form of Hopkins's poetry with its emotion and religious vision"[12].

His obsession with Hopkins is both obvious and revealing, where the poet's divine rapture is translated by Said into a form of sublimation:

> It is in the poetry of Hopkins that we find a very pure performance of … an omni-sexuality transferred from natural to literary life, underpinning the entire career and text. I use Hopkins precisely because his sexual imagery plays itself out generally in the writing project and moves particularly at first in correspondence with his own consecrated celibacy. His poetry is launched in order to confirm, in repetition, a divine metaphysic of creation, a metaphysic of beginning and creating.[13]

Some of the sexual anxiety evident in Said's poetry—and it arises (mostly cryptically) more than once—finds its counterpart here. The spirituality to which he gives voice, although hardly what we associate with Said's writing or politics, was not confined to Hopkins. In a graduate essay on the seventeenth-century poet Richard Crashaw, he expresses his "immediate affinity" with these "urgent contemplative poems … It is not far-fetched to seek the following analogy in the Mass: ritual symbols are operative complements of the spiritual drama they inform and develop"[14].

Whether or not Said's verses are meant to perform a spiritual drama, they are certainly psychologically revealing. They chart with startling emotion the doubts of a man torn by a native culture with which he is at times disappointed, projecting onto it a modernity whose sophistication lies in resisting the West while acknowledging its guilty attractions. With the exception of "The Castle", composed at Mt. Hermon in 1951 when Said was sixteen (and still new to his American home), most of the poems in this volume were likely composed between 1956 and 1968—a period extending from his late college years through graduate school and into his early years as a young professor at Columbia. He published some of his poetry in *Al-Kulliyah* ("the college", the Alumni journal of the American University of Beirut) during the gap year he spent in Cairo between college and graduate school while working in his father's business. Unsure about his future, and certainly contemplating (among other things) a life as a professional writer, the poems at times allude sarcastically to the world of business and with affection to the tactility of Cairene everyday life. It was a period in which he was reading through all of the poetry of W. H. Auden, "puzzling through Kierkegaard and Nietzsche", reading Freud, and writing music criticism, some of which he published.[15] Whatever else—and there are a number of surprisingly elegant, crafted lines—his poetry can be recognized as exploring his Middle Eastern setting, his mixed relationships with family, the ambiguities of his first marriage, and his deep investments in classical music. Several of the poems, in fact, likely date from his year in Cairo before entering Harvard, and to the period immediately after—his first years in graduate school before his scholarly studies overwhelm him, and move him towards the public intellectual that we know today.

If often more antique in their feel than we might expect, the poems are distinctive on several grounds, and always interesting. They offer insights, at any rate, into the personality of the author of *Orientalism*, *The World, the Text and the Critic*, and *Culture & Imperialism* to a degree hidden in those works themselves. "The Castle", for instance, as juvenilia, has shades of Tennyson, if Tennyson had read Kafka or studied Fanon. The occasionally archaic diction itself—"edulcorate", "engirdling", "perd", "bosky", "chainéd", "plish"– seem less a failing than an attempt to mimic the stilted idiom of a colonial education. It is a poetry marked by obscure references, offering a glimpse into Said's ornate mental repertoire—"Hans von Bulow", "Galatea", "Cosima Wagner", "Pleyel pianos", "Antar"—and they are swarmed by an orientalist imagery of "baladis", "Saracens", "scimitars", "deserts", "nomad's robes", "clay idols", "Crusaders", "mountain shepherds", and "lucent veils". Considering the emphasis in Said's critical work on space and place and the political importance of geography, it is less surprising to see the luxuriant evocation of a specific topography of dusty roads, grottoes, plump figtrees, desert flowers, muddy clods, and the "beckoning hands of lambent hills". Most revealing of all, perhaps, is the poems' tendency to see the world through musical form. Musical imagery is everywhere, testifying to how much of Said's mind in an introspective mood was immersed in the sounds, forms, and fables of Western classical music.

With one exception ("The Castle"), the poems here are taken in manuscript form, both hand-written and typed, from the Edward Said papers at Columbia University.[16] Several of the poems exist in more than one form, with subtle variants between the different versions. I have chosen those that appeared to be latest, most complete, or best-expressed.

Timothy Brennan
—August 2023

1. Perhaps because so often it was not poetry written in English. His work on modern Arabic poetry for the *TLS* in 1976 and for the Beirut-based modernist journal *Mawaqif* on the modernity of Arabic poetry complement a larger task for which he is not always recognized: promoting the publication and dissemination of contemporary Arab writing.
2. Edward W. Said papers, Columbia University, 83:1:III.1.
3. R. P. Blackmur, *A Primer of Ignorance*, ed. Joseph Frank (1940; New York: Harcourt, Brace & World, 1967), 20.
4. Ibid. 60.
5. R. P. Blackmur, *Language as Gesture: Essays in Poetry* (1935; New York: Harcourt, Brace and Company, 1952), 3.
6. Ibid. 372.
7. David Lehman, letter to author, 10 May 2018.
8. George Makdisi, “Inquiry into the Origins of Humanism”, in Asma Afsaruddin and A. H. Mathias Zahniser (eds.), *Humanism, Culture & Language in the Near East: Studies in Honor of Georg Krotkoff* (Winona Lake, IN: Eisenbrauns, 1997), 19.
9. Even in the case of Swift, although Said delves into his prose (above all, *A Tale of a Tub*), his published writing is mostly about Swift’s political texts and his poetry. See “Swift’s Tory Anarchy”, *Eighteenth-Century Studies* (Fall 1969), 3/1: 48–66. Hussein the “ironic Palestinian poet” is one of two to whom Said dedicates *The Question of Palestine* (1979).
10. His dissertation co-director, Monroe Engel, won the Bowdoin prize in his senior year at Harvard for an essay on Hopkins.
11. Edward W. Said, *Beginnings: Intention and Method* (Baltimore: Johns Hopkins UP, 1975), 256–7
12. Edward W. Said papers, Columbia University, 28:9:II.
13. Edward W. Said papers, Columbia University, 97:20:III.1.
14. Edward W. Said papers, Columbia University, 81:1: III.1—under “General Notes, undated, 1957”.
15. Edward W. Said, *Out of Place: A Memoir* (New York: Vintage, 1999), 287.
16. Edward W. Said papers, Columbia University 77:32:II.4 and 81:1:III.1.

Songs of an Eastern Humanist

The Castle

High on its craggy mountain top,
Stands the symbol of power and might.
Through countless years it has stood there,
Defiant and proud as one whose
Strength and will has made him
Feared, even though unloved,
For fear and love seldom go hand in hand.
Its walls, now beginning to crumble,
But still as enduring as ever,
Covered with crawling, twisting, and turning ivy;
Ivy like a serpent, always seeking to crush the life
Out of its erstwhile foe.
Towers, of gray and crude stone,
Pinnacles of glory and triumph,
As once Crusaders brave, with their
Banners of flaming red and white,
Didst survey the motley Saracen host
With arrogant and contemptuous glance.
There once, inside its massive portals
Did laughs of gay revelries of flighty men and women,
And harsh screams from the dungeons foul,
Echo together in terrible discord;
A true symphony of discordance and ever approaching doom.
But gone now are days of pleasure and horror,
For, here instead has Dame Decay put her abrasive and
all-encompassing hand
As if to quell the sustaining power of her rival.
In a burst of strength the castle didst try,
But in vain, to shake off this leech-like grip.
Today, it stands,
To all outward and careless observers, still
A threatening giant, with weapons brandished and ready;
Internally, a labyrinth, and mire-like
Cave of corruption and rot.
Where Nature's powers of destruction,
Are at work—eating, eating, eating
Away at its stone walls and doors,
That all shall perish and crumble
As a clay idol into dust.

(1951–2)

We have strayed into an ambiance made edulcorate,
The doors of our hearts flung open to the humming dawn
Where amber turrets break the mimicking light into patches,
Level fields, many-sided, worn through as if by hurrying boys.
And now, if memory could entertain us into past effluence,
There would, I think, be music, sonority held by us
With Dante, majestic still point, the double flame, timbrels
And harps, rising all, broad-backed from
Quiet shores. The gifts of twenty pastimes, marshalled, plump
Fig trees on a soft hillside, have tempted forty like us;
But the blooms of desert flowers are realest at noon
When warm sands murmur glees with the loitering ice,
A tenuous syntax harrowed finally to silence by stronger
warmth:
And the walk of lovers continues easily in the contented air.

An eager Levantine twilight swallows the sun
And the hand that stretched forward lost itself
In impeccable blankness where paths flounder
Along the tramontane wastes, then lifts,
Lifts and shapes a choreographic freshness
To be ready for a noon that will not come
When sight stops, sounds remain, telling
A sharp performance of swift riddles and quibbles;
They in their turn to be gobbled by ravenous ears.
But this is an East that does not know of cycles
Of massive futilities, before, ended at once—
Those freed from their source only to nuzzle closer
Like merry leeches fed on a fragrant history.
In the night of silent books and emptied studies,
Readers itch the street with the slippered shuffles,
peering into windows
At strung-across dolls mashing tin words with shaking
and waving
"We are, we must, we will, we can, we are, we must."
The tin words are dangled with the suspended bulbs,
Worshipful effigies expected to melt away years of fuzz,
While dirty gray-brown women are stained at their breasts
With many little mouths, crying for what is theirs.
There are green trees, and yellow buds, a fat nature
Snoring a sow-like sleep away, down far into the muddy clods.

The early morning gently forges our city's sounds
Into that attended pitch of gallant diffidence
That, standing away from studious violence
Melts its voices in the wave that surrounds.
The sellers of bread and fruit, of meat and milk
Merchants on bicycles, carts and camels
Jingle the clouds, even the sullen sun's enamel,
Shakes them to selling, robbing the veil of silk.
Hussein, Mohammed, Ali, Ahmed, Mahmoud and Aziz—
Arose the men of names that were strands even to Cadiz,
The flock of pieties that made of water, ice, of ice sherbet
To drink in the cooler summer's night along with kismet.

Requiem

For priceless waves of unremitting feeling
Washing over the fragments of a forlorn beach
There may have been a man seeking announcement
Of boiled sorrow, somewhere, in the depths of
His soul that mirrored the rushing speed, now
Worried with backward gales and forward tides,
Now rising to kiss ragged patches of lucent veils,
Clouds in an orient streaked with mottled grief;
A turn-about of stars flashed its haughty beams
With hidden clingings, elusive in fogs of a larger transience
Ever sidling to the graves of previous lovers,
Unquiet, and blazoned across gaps of shaded
Worried chasms in which little life dared.
Grottoes of a lank enemy screaming derisively in
Tremulous anguish—There is no mercy here, mercy here
Is away, lost in the wastes of careening space
Heavens that have fallen to frothy curses
In a remote night whose sad litanies are
Dust in the dreams of an empty waste;
The Cold, beckoning hands of lambent hills.

Desert Flowers

I.

The primitive yawn of a desert dawn
Unyielding, eternal smile of lone grief,
Heralds a small-scale mock dies irae.
Locked in a bosom, arid but brighter
Than the sun's image on a scimitar,
Stands the past's waste, rich in moody frenzy,
Impassioned prison of our humane dreams.
The present is sickly, pale, an effect
Rehearsed and taught, but imperfectly nice,
Just as pretty as a shop-worn bouquet
Of wax blossoms. There is no future here,
Time's tether completed, eaten away
By the ridiculous vermin of hope—
A sterile vision fraught with rhythmic cant,
Decisive, but frighteningly restrained.

II.

The nomad's exhortation
Rose in defiance
Of a swirling dusty wrath.
His striped tents were
Bristling targets, mute and drab
Bathed in a banal
Sad forlornness matching the
Unimaginative folds
Of the nomad's robe.
Ragged woolen animals,
Toys on the harshness
Of a godless continent
Of flint and gritty
Terror, belched their plaintive cries
In an agony
Of irresponsible fright.
The whole: a picture composed with the self-conscious artistry
Of a merciless scorpion encircling its prey, poised now
For the engirdling kiss of fluid triumphant poison.

III.

The pointed beat of tiny drums
The dragging sway of unripe dates
Upon the honied brown
Of sandy lakes;

A lovely plish,
A mute sweep of the eyes,
A scooping hand
Straining without malice;

Here was a clean purity,
Above and apart,
Yet sunk in the recurrent
Mirage of an open city
Shining with kind eyes
On the wide honest plain.

Vision's Haze

An evening past in Hamana's shade—
The water blessed the dusty rock
In jubilant rivulets, chattering silver verses
Of tried, endless wisdom, near and in
An earth never scarred with smudged campaigns
That betoken regret and sorrow.

A mountain shepherd slipped in sight
Braided to his reed flute in love;

Time and the world limp past:
Hamana's refulgence, permanent fluidity
Without purpose or contour, beyond hieroglyphs
Beyond regret and sorrow.

The finest hour of my life
Was, it was, there is no doubt
Upon that creaky seat
In Music Hall.
On it I heard the flutist blow
One blast and off they all went
Some blew, some pulled, some didn't
But I was caught in the middle
And

Old People of the Village

Hamdy and Khadija together were withered now.
Their children, mostly dead or away, their friends dead.
Men annoyed them, women
Bored them
Children were hateful wounds, like
Unfinished dreams of the way they couldn't grow.
Perfectly dressed in spotless robes their younger
Village mates wore for feasts; Khadija and Hamdy
Never went to feasts, never shared a meal,
Never received, never gave, rarely moved.
We heard their cracked voices behind a cracked door
Soothing each other in lulling bleats and squeals
Of times when Hamdy could have been Antar.

Wistful Music

Night in time, day without
And I fled with my heart's
Roof torn open, blown apart
As I might not stop, neither
Running nor the flying-wide
Shelter, once fast, now not.
A far cadence in soft whites
And blues, blew flickering circles
Round the way; the billows
Couched to memory, for heart's
Aroused, a cast of entrancement,
The lull that invites, silent Siren,
Opium dust, wafted waves, chords
Resolved. As moved we on
Previous blows, impulses bared
To simple beauties, power-bearing,
Hush-born, asked in fact,
What were those chainéd rings
Of sounds: perfect once, broken
To admit, to make sight in blind,
Close, shelter—hearts and no
Ringing to answer, yes.

Windy corners and empty corridors are trying perds:
For the last witness of lost commerce
Is a trunk half smashed
And half tottering with the fires of sand.
Blessed with blind opacity,
Dotted with red brands by forgotten demons
A gurgling half-tone creeps on:
Mysterious snakes and whips
Small scourges of a vast memory—
And the vacancy of my dream,
Glimmers.

Retrospect

The world does not tell its time from the east
Where crashing noises mix with silly bleats
And the sun's rays imprison as in modal rounds.
Then a great longing was brought painfully forth
Defying bosky mists of a far-off north, mists
That to their natives looked like russet brows—
Still, diversity of vision was not for the east.
For the safer men—but there were few alive.
Longing was a simple dream from which to awake
And sing the destined sounds, refreshed, louder.
Ours was not a safe view for we clamored for new harmonies,
Carrying in them an opulent new fate, perhaps not ours—
But who was strong enough for second thoughts, and songs.

A Celebration in Three Movements

I.

She had retraced the way of painless joy
Beyond which I could not see;
The grace of her beauty shed the ages of repetition
With the effortlessness and impersonality of frictionless motion.
The guiding music of impassioned souls were also
The colours of her spirit: dancing, laughing, energised.
And those who knew her loved her: her disciples
Wafted forward pitilessly on the waves her fulfillment.
The subjects of thought sunk in a desert of trees and
lush bushes
Struggled in a hiding of euphoric joy or overcome
Unseen, but endlessly present and felt shapes—or,
They may have been animals, souls, or strands—
Jaded and academic in the hold they had, surrounding
Her presence, these subjects of our thought,
The wholeness of a tightly interfused man
Rolled, rolls through the sidespreading jam of experience:
Identities, presences and even lights peered through,
Begged for their release, their only possible ransom
A strength either unknown or uncreated.
She was, I insist, she insisted, a lovely thorn
Growing where angels had left a now perverted fertility;
Demonic growth, cells of fervent love tearing the average
emotional income
Into fragments of questioning shadows: a chant of regular
rhythm
Went up: give us light, glue, and a ruler,
Light, glue and a ruler.

II.

The shimmering lake surface, blazoned,
A patch on the dusty, round-topped map,
Breathed its life in an ineffable tranquility.

She was barefoot that day—
The world limped along behind her
Scarred, where she was perfect and taut.

It was strange and fearful—
Trees, granite and robins
Upset by a positive pole, expectant—swaying and gloomy.

Mercy was the whiteness of her skin,
Hazel the depth of her regard
And grey the haze of doubt.

The act itself was sudden but fair,
Strong and careful—weak and pretty;
No one played “judge”—for the present is too fast for thought.

Dressed, lethargic, determined—
The grammar of defeat imposed upon
The passion of romance—spent, fallen.

III.

Composed into a benign certainty
Swathed in a soft glow of nostalgic musing
Rose a perfect shape of crystalline elegance
It was a tremendous effort to patch and piece
Criss and cross, cut and paste,
Yet all Galateas give pleasure—and this Product
was no exception.
Of course the common frenzy of creation may have cooled,
The heat of passion that had spent itself a lot earlier,
May have been, it is true, too carefully itemized;
But symphonies and epics don't grow on trees.
We were told of perspiration, garrets and dedications.
Yet the filthy backwash of an age of spontaneous generation
Bathed us in wind and ooze, washed our ills in grime and soot.
Sit you down and create, that is all—
Buy all you need at the corner store—light, glue, ruler.
And still the same questions remain: what are the yardsticks
of emotion?
The imbroglios of our fevered minds press further in,
Diagnose, substantiate, piece together, then relax.
The store salesman tells a modern parable:
"Tired soul, tired heart, or tired mind? Let us know.
We sell patent remedies for all ailments. And then,
Why, and then you'll feel good, real good.
Don't lose faith or hope, there's a solution for everything."
I have a friend who plays with memory
Just as a child plays the harmonica, delighted
With the bizarre cacophony of jumbled sounds.
This is the music of life lived in a bottle label.
Reach for a hope drug brother; our greatest virtue
Is the kinship and common mediocrity, ready made
clothes to fit us all.
We could jump into the pond of esoterics
Or the teacup of rebellion,
But the battle of knowledge must be fought in the sea of jam
In silk suits and space helmets.

Little Transformation

Force away, cajoling
She writes of a kind song,
Tuned in the halcyon scale
And branded thus: affection

Smarting with salt,
Wrapped in a shredded leaf,
A shoeless holiday in fantasy
Scarred but ever—bright.

Careful alloy of ups-and-ins
Dropped through molasses and cotton,
Palatable, sticky, clinging
And now enter: chicanery

One attention, one rapt century of feeling,
And the fasting eyes and body
Had no power to blame or creep;
There was no complaint from slight content
In shady orchards of a half perfect fruit.
I have regarded that now with unbelief,
Deep in the trembling reaches of forgetfulness
Asking what it was that ran through
Without finding a face to stop the chasm.
The blesséd heat wrapped my thoughts like limbs
Soaked and soothed with precious care, softly
Resilient in halls of glistening shadows.
And at last my crested roads rose up,
Animate waves along a smoothéd map
Where flights of birds heraldic fling
An open, open air their charméd selves.

The top of my heart flung its doors apart
In the moonlight of an exquisite wave,
Sonorous, and the light breathed with tone
As my arms awakened the air to passion,
Fierce beauty, unstilled into the calm of eastern skies.

Now the movement of princes rises the earth,
And trumpets brandished in lyric splendor,
Naught is hurt in the wake of their efforts,
Curtains of an old ritual that had no end,
Youth apprehended glory despite unlovely promises.

We had cried together in conquered fields
Where no one else had been,
The morning greeted no one,
Site of an ancient temple
Moved our hand linked thoughts,
For we glided away in tremors;
One gaiety begged for a caress
But we heeded not, and
Down we floated on stark receptacles

Hans von Bulow in Cairo

Heard, no, but hurt most certainly,
The old tonesmith could never bandy *baladi*—
Now *that's* music to Arab ears—
So, like Cosima's satin slippers (her bunioned, round feet
Were so tired), his shoes gathered the dust
As Beethoven's priest he'd shaken off, angered the king,
Found Cairo, saw his end, suffered the dust, and—
The Coptic couple come and go, saying only hallo, hallo—
Filled his memory's palace's sand bottom with unsifted sound.
Artin the Armenian, Horus the Hamite,
Sursock the Syrian, Djenan his unused study's genie,
Standing on a shady veranda corner promised his past
Glory to present, and the line of his interest dipped,
The sun slowed the time, a string-dandled doll fell there.
Eugenie's (the Empress's) adorned Pleyel, still there,
trundled by Yusif Bey,
Tempted with a silky Brahms but only broke the silence's back;
Bulow's wordless, gleaming fury goes along, along, along,
Mounting the hot air and spreads, like a burnished gong,
Across his inner sky, to which the sacred Nile
With only a muddy-veined delta proffered, homages.
Ah Richard, there is no love in death.

Song of an Eastern Humanist

The ruffianly dust blew whorls and mist
In secret hiding-places whose air was a tryst,
And old men told their beads with mine
What a way to appease the muses, a furious nine.
Then I tumbled from a curious perch
Flailing fronds and, in avid search,
A bent fellow trailing the file,
Picking what others, whose wile
Had flown circumambient
In methodic dodges sapient,
To be, to remain what I will,
A roguish elegist, the Arabic Till.
The carol flows, the lyric twangs,
Plump, armless, losing fangs.